27.92

D1391379

CB

A Passion for Asparagus

Chris Sheehan

A Passion for Asparagus

By Chris Sheehan

Published in 2007 by
Word4Word

www.eveshamasparagus.co.uk

ISBN10: 0-9551677-8-7
ISBN13 978-0-9551677-8-2

Produced by Word4Word
Design & Publishing Ltd,
Evesham, UK
www.w4wdp.com

Printed by Cromwell Press,
Trowbridge, UK

A Passion for Asparagus

Dedicated to Fur

Michael J.B

Contents

Preparing Asparagus for Market, Michael Barnard

List of Recipes

Introduction

Do you get excited about asparagus? You may be the kind of person who is fed up with all-round 'seasonal produce', or perhaps you're concerned about the food miles that your asparagus has flown from Peru (typically 7000). Or maybe you just enjoy the colour or feel of a bunch of asparagus. If so, this book is for you.

The taste of freshly cut and boiled or steamed asparagus with fresh butter is a sublime reminder of all that is good about locally grown, seasonal produce. Perhaps you yearn for a simpler time before the domination of supermarkets or you may be simply looking for a different way of cooking your favourite vegetable. For those of you who love good food and are interested in where it comes from, read on and learn why this special vegetable deserves all the care and nurturing that goes into bringing it to your table.

Perhaps you have picked this book up out of curiosity. Many people think asparagus is expensive and intimidating to prepare and cook. This book will dispel some of the myths and formality and show you ways of enjoying this superb vegetable simply.

The people who have contributed to this book are the growers and market gardeners; the publicans and chefs; and of course the local characters who all have something to say about gras as it is known in the Vale of Evesham.

The story of Evesham asparagus today highlights the growing dichotomy in British farming and retailing. On the one hand are the supermarkets, which account for 80% of all fruit and vegetables bought. The supermarkets and those who supply them have been cast as the demons, who pursue uniformity and cost-effective distribution at the expense of taste and regionality. On the other hand are the small local growers selling their freshly cut crop by the roadside.

However, it is too easy to castigate supermarkets when most of us have neither the time nor the inclination to shop in local farm shops and farmers' markets all of the time. Indeed, many country stores offer limited choice of over-priced, often not-very-fresh fruit and veg. And so while we may aspire to low food miles, organic produce or the Slow Food Movement, we have to accept commercial growing because of the choice it offers.

The large commercial growers, who have hundreds of acres of asparagus fields have highly efficient systems for getting their produce on to our tables, often in less than 36 hours. And while the food purist may not like buying Peruvian asparagus in the winter months, it would be going too far to insist our local farm shop does not stock it.

At the other end of the spectrum is the discovery of a freshly cut round of asparagus at a road-side stall in the heart of the Vale of Evesham, knowing that a precious supper is in prospect in the early British summer.

This book is not a history book although it contains interviews and vignettes from those who have lived in and grown asparagus around the Vale of Evesham and beyond. It is about asparagus in the 21st century where good comes from both ends of the retailing spectrum. Indeed many large commercial growers have their own mission and passion – that is to reduce costs so that it becomes an everyday choice. For a vegetable that costs around £7-8 per kilo (compared to 40p per kilo for carrots for example), asparagus is certainly a vegetable for the well-off (unless grown in the garden) and probably explains why only 5% of the British population have ever eaten it.

Nor is this book a horticultural manual, although the growing, harvesting and presentation of gras has a fascinating history.

The story of asparagus today is about its specialness and how it would remain special even if the price were to come down to that of the Brussel sprout. For it is here that the eccentricity of British life is still to be found. It may lie in the bottle of asparagus liqueur proudly stocked at the unique Evesham Hotel or in the character of David Caswell who, as one of the few remaining blacksmiths, still makes asparagus knives used in the harvesting of the tender spears. Asparagus

attracts attention because of its rare seasonality in an age of strawberries at Christmas and new potatoes all year around.

Asparagus has been vested with many properties over the years. Some medicinal, some aphrodisiac and these are explored too.

Reading about asparagus is too vicarious a pleasure for all but the hardened enthusiast so I hope this book will help to encourage a more practical enjoyment of the crop through one of its recipes, gleaned from locals and professional chefs alike. They have been selected not to be representative or exhaustive but to illustrate some unusual but not too gimmicky ways to prepare the fresh crop.

While focusing on English and mainly Evesham asparagus, many other countries celebrate and revere their local crop - from white asparagus in Germany to the vast fields of the crops of California and Peru – these are worthy of mention here too.

Like the Italian *campanilista* who swears that their local produce is best, this book has been written with a similar passion and is dedicated to those who share this emotion.

'You needn't tell me that a man who doesn't love oysters and asparagus and good wines has got a soul, or a stomach either. He's simply got the instinct for being unhappy.'

'Saki', pen name of Scottish writer Hector Hugh Munro (1870-1916)

Asparagus with Hollandaise

**32 spears of
Asparagus**
**225g of unsalted
butter**
**2 tsps of white
wine vinegar**
**1 tsp. of cracked
white pepper**
4 egg yolks
Salt
Lemon juice

SERVES 4 AS A STARTER

Stagg Inn, Titley, Kington,
Herefordshire, UK

Hollandaise

Melt the butter in a small pan over a low heat until it foams. Spoon off the foam and leave butter to settle.

Boil vinegar with pepper and pinch of salt. Remove from heat. Add two tbs. of water and the egg yolks. Whisk over a bain-marie until the egg yolks are light and creamy, 6-8 minutes. Whisking continually gently pour in the butter. Add lemon juice and salt to taste. Put to one side to keep warm.

Asparagus

Chop off woody ends approx. 1/3 of each spear. Peel the stem with a potato peeler. Drop spears into a large saucepan of boiling salted water, cook until tips are tender, 2-4 minutes. Although soggy asparagus is undesirable, if the asparagus is too *al dente* it can taste bitter.

To serve, arrange asparagus in the centre of a warmed plate pour sauce over.

'When good British asparagus is in season there is absolutely nothing like it.'

Jamie Oliver

Asparagus Baked in Milk

SERVES 4
2 lbs asparagus
1 teaspoon sugar
1 quantity milk
sauce (made with
milk, butter, flour
and nutmeg)
1 tablespoon butter
2 tablespoons
breadcrumbs
Salt to taste

The Best of Ukrainian
Cuisine, Expanded Edition,
Bohdan Zahny

ISBN 0781806542, 1994,
Published by Hippocrene
Books, Inc New York

Wash asparagus, remove tough scales and bottom portions. Cut asparagus in 1 inch pieces and place in pot with hot water. Add sugar and cook for 15-30 minutes. Drain. Place in casserole and cover with milk sauce. Sprinkle with bread crumbs and drizzle with butter. Bake at 350° F for 40 minutes.

History

The edible tender shoots of this succulent member of the Lily family have been valued over the centuries from the time of the Ancient Greeks. The Greek scientist and pharmacologist, Dioscorides, used it to treat liver and kidney disorders.

The unique flavour, appearance and properties of asparagus led to its widespread cultivation by the Romans after they discovered it growing wild. Pliny mentions a variety growing near Ravenna in 200 BC and records various details of its cultivation in Rome including its weight per stem.

It was eaten fresh and dried or frozen for winter consumption. Chariots took it to the snows of the Alps before it was consumed in an Epicurean feast. The most choice buds were even shipped across the Roman Empire in specially designated boats. Indeed Emperor Caesar Augustus explained the term 'haste' to his subordinates with the phrase 'do it quicker than you can cook asparagus' (*Citius quam asparagi coquentur*).

Asparagus is depicted in ancient Egyptian writings and it has also been grown in Syria and Spain since ancient times.

Elsewhere American Indians dried it for medicinal use, especially for its diuretic properties.

In the 16th century, asparagus gained popularity in France, particularly with the Huguenots. A variety is named after the Argenteuil region, where it is still grown. The French Huguenots, settling around London supposedly started the market garden culture system. Battersea was most famous for the earliest and best asparagus and by the end of the 18th century there were 260 acres of gardens mainly cropped with asparagus.

From England, the early colonists took it to America. It is reported that early colonists in

Virginia were eating hothouse asparagus in 1773.

Asparagus is often called the 'food of kings'. King Louis XIV of France was so fond of this delicacy that he ordered special greenhouses built so he could enjoy asparagus all year-round!

With its growing popularity, asparagus became the subject of several paintings by Frans Snyders (1613), Snyder and Rubens (1608) and later Manet (1880). In the Snyder and Rubens painting, the bundle of asparagus appears with green buds, tinged with purple, looking much like today's vegetable.

In the mid-17th Century, the diarist Pepys bought a bundle of 'sparrow-grass' in Fenchurch Street, London for 1s 6d (7.5p).

A bumper crop!

Preparing asparagus rounds

' **Playwrights are like**

men who have been

dining for a month in

an Indian restaurant.

After eating curry

night after night, they

deny the existence of

asparagus. '

Peter Ustinov (actor)

History of Cultivation in Evesham

The spread of the city pushed asparagus cultivation out into the countryside and by the 1700s it was being grown at Evesham and had spread to Badsey (known locally as Backsey) and surrounding districts. In 1799, Worcestershire seed sellers were offering a variety called Large Green Battersea. Evesham asparagus is mentioned in J. C. Loudon's famous Encyclopaedia Of Gardening published in 1824. In fact there are records to show that asparagus was grown in Evesham as early as 1782 when a crop failure affected towns such as Bath and Bristol.

By 1870 other areas in Cambridgeshire, Lancashire and Devon took up the cultivation. The area around Formby became a significant growing area, as recorded in a National Trust archive, perhaps stimulated by the need for high-quality produce for the ocean liners setting sail from nearby Liverpool.

Why is asparagus localised in certain areas in the UK and elsewhere? And is Evesham asparagus the best? Each area of cultivation will have a view on this, especially those by the coasts with sandier soils. Like wine production, there are a range of factors such as climate, variety of rootstock, cropping cycle and soil or terroir that influence the finished product.

The cultivation of asparagus in Badsey's clay soils, rather than the typical sandy soil elsewhere, may be the magic ingredient that locals claim makes their gras special. Before 1880, asparagus markets were held in the streets. In that year, auctions began at Evesham's market square run by Urwick and Hunt of Ludlow.

The history of asparagus marketing has some fascinating anecdotes. The railways were an important part of opening up new markets and in 1852 a new station opened up at Evesham. However, growers were not happy with the charges levied and delays were frequent. One grower lost all his consignment in a fire and was charged for the cost of the railway carriage! Asparagus, as a high value crop, was one of the few to be carefully packed in hampers or 'flats' as they were known. Unlike other crops, asparagus was unique in that it was not carried in goods trains but in the guard's van of passenger trains!

Throughout the 20th century asparagus growing declined, especially during the 1960s and 70s. Acreages have significantly declined – in the early years of the last century there were almost 1500 acres under cultivation in the UK. In Bretforton alone 240 acres were used for asparagus cultivation. Now, in the village, the figure is less than 10.

A sketch by Michael Barnard, a local artist and historian in the Vale of Evesham, showing

Gras cutters saluting the RAF, Michael Barnard

asparagus cutting during the war, forms the basis of an insight into the importance of agriculture in wartime. The cartoon shows a Havard plane flying over asparagus fields with the gras cutters saluting the RAF. He says: 'During the war years, even the threat of invasion did not deter the Home Guard from cutting asparagus in the month of May and into June. Attendance on parade was in Battalion Orders of No 6 Platoon, Broadway Company Home Guard'. The copy of the original order reads: 'In view of the difficulties of attending parade during the asparagus season for some members, the rule regarding attendance given in Routine Orders No. 32 on May 2nd is postponed for one month.'

The war was perhaps one of the reasons that the acreage under cultivation declined. During the war, cultivated land was at a premium and 'luxury crops' such as flowers and asparagus were reduced or abandoned in favour of crops such as onions or carrots.

Asparagus soldiers

'You needn't tell me that a man who doesn't love oysters and asparagus and good wines has got a soul, or a stomach either. He's simply got the instinct for being unhappy.'

'Saki', pen name of Scottish writer
Hector Hugh Munro (1870-1916)

'Of all the plants of the garden, it receives the most praiseworthy care – nature has made the Asparagus wild, so that anyone may gather as found.'

Pliny

Asparagus and New Potatoes Avgolemono

This is a spring dish of subtle delicacy and exquisite flavour. The gentle cooking method allows the potatoes to absorb a muted asparagus flavour, the vegetables are lightly coated with the classic avgolemono sauce. Serve as an elegant first course, lunch or as an accompaniment to grilled or roasted meats.

16 small new potatoes (about 675 g/1½ lbs), peeled if desired and cut into halves or quarters.
675 g/1½lbs asparagus
2 large eggs
Strained juice of 2 lemons
Sea salt and freshly ground white pepper to taste

FOR SERVING
Small sprigs of fresh chervil or flat leaf parsley

Flavours of Greece
Rosemary Barron
ISBN 1-902304-28 4
2000
Published by Grubb Street
London

SERVES 4

Fill an asparagus steamer or large 2-handled saucepan two thirds full with lightly salted water and bring to a boil. Add the potatoes, cover and boil for 15 minutes, or until barely tender.

Meanwhile, break off the tough ends of the stalks at the point where they snap easily. Rinse the asparagus and tie in 2 bundles with kitchen string, leaving enough string on each to loop over the handles of the saucepan. When the potatoes are almost cooked, balance the asparagus in the saucepan, the stalks immersed in boiling water. Loop the string firmly around the handles so the asparagus tips remain above the surface to steam. Cover and cook for 4 minutes.

While the asparagus cooks, beat the eggs with a hand whisk or electric mixer until pale and frothy, about 2 minutes. Gradually add the lemon juice and whisk 1 minute longer. Drain the vegetables in a colander set over a bowl and keep warm. Gradually whisk 175 ml/6 fl oz of the cooking liquid into the egg mixture. Transfer to the top of a double boiler set over hot water and cook over a low heat, stirring with a wooden spoon, until the sauce thickens enough to lightly coat the back of the spoon, about 1 minute.

Arrange the vegetables on a warm platter and sprinkle with salt and pepper. Pour over the sauce, garnish with the chervil, and serve at once.

27. *Asparagaceae*

Asparagus officinalis L.   Gemeiner Spar

Properties

Description and names: *Asparagus officinalis L* (*Liliaceae-Asparagacease*) is part of a large genus of some 300 species. Many of its cousins are tough climbers found in Asia and Africa but with fleshy and edible young stems. *A. acutifolius L* is eaten in Spain and Turkey.

Asparagus comes in green, purple, white or somewhere in-between, with our European neighbours cultivating the white variant. White asparagus is grown in the dark, with earth piled up over the spears to prevent it from developing a green colour.

The name comes from classical Latin. Medieval Latin called it *sparagus* hence the old English name sperage. The Latin has been corrupted to 'sparrow grass' and locally around Evesham it is simply known as gras (pronounced *grass* unlike the French word for fat). John Walker in 1791 stated that using the full name of asparagus 'had an air of stiffness and pedantry' (see Folklore on page 35 for more on names). Even today it is easily recognised in Latin languages (asperge (French), Spargel (German), asperge (Dutch), espárrago (Spanish).

Aphrodisiac Properties

Asparagus has several properties, real and imagined, that add to the mystique of this special vegetable. Many foods are reputed to be aphrodisiacs and this seems to be as much associated with their high cost at nice restaurants as with any established science. Perhaps the logic is that if he or she thinks that much of me when it comes to the credit card then they must really fancy me – and such passion is always a turn-on.

Asparagus officinalis
Ex libris Kurt Stubers online library

'The last thing I want to
do is cause loads of hype
or problems, I just want
to go in there and get my
asparagus or whatever.'

Prince William

Nicholas Culpepper the famous herbalist (1616–1654) was quoted as saying that asparagus 'stirs up lust in man and woman'.

Various writings try to find a scientific basis for its aphrodisiac properties but these are based more on wishful thinking than on good science. Potassium, Vitamin

A and folic acid are all cited as being responsible, whether in stimulating the glands, overcoming inability to reach orgasm or as a raw material for the sex hormones.

It is reported that in 19th-century France, bridegrooms were required to eat several courses of asparagus because of its reputation to arouse.

One erotic image of asparagus is the eating of the phallic-spears with melting butter placed seductively between the lips. Not unlike a savoury take on the 1970s Cadbury Flake™ adverts.

In the erotic work *The Perfumed Garden* written in the 16th century by Shaykh al Nefzawi, we find this statement: 'He who boils asparagus and then fries them in fat, and then pours upon them the yolks of eggs with pounded condiments, and eats every day of this dish, will grow very strong for the coitus, and find in it a stimulant for his amorous desires'. I am not sure that the washing up would have the same effect though!

Is there any evidence of asparagus' aphrodisiac properties? Several scientific studies show that extracts of various asparagus species in fact have a contraceptive effect rather than promoting pregnancy!

The
Asparagus
Festival
Bretforton
Worcestershire
2006

Truffle Cappuccino with Parmesan Crisps

**Two rounds of
Asparagus
Olive Oil, a drizzle
Malden Sea
Salt, a pinch
Cracked Black
Pepper, a pinch
White Truffle Oil
or Oil infusion
Milk ¼ pint
Fresh grated
Parmesan**

SERVES **4**

Dominic Pattin
Head Chef
Cottage in the Wood Hotel,
Great Malvern,
Worcestershire, UK

Dominic Pattin writes: 'I feel that fresh asparagus has such a wonderful delicate taste it should not be spoilt by lots of added ingredients. This recipe lets you savour the taste and the foam compliments the asparagus.'

Parmesan crisps: On a baking sheet place a pastry cutter on parchment paper, sprinkle in grated cheese to form a round. Bake until golden. The crisp can be shaped over a rolling pin.

Asparagus: Heat a griddle pan and drizzle with olive oil. Add asparagus, turn during cooking. Asparagus is cooked when stem gives a little when pinched.

Cappuccino: Infuse milk with truffle or oil infusion, season with salt and pepper, froth with a hand blender.

Place asparagus on serving plate, place froth only from your cappuccino onto the asparagus and garnish with crisps.

Bon appetite!

'I grew up with asparagus and the taste of it is part of my childhood'

Rachel Green

Smelly Urine and Other Body Fluids!

One of asparagus' most distinctive properties is the production of sulphurous compounds on digestion, which produces a distinctive smell in urine soon after its consumption. It is asparagusic acid that is responsible (or alpha-aminodimethyl-gamma-butyrothetin for those of a chemical mind). This is found in asparagus and a few other food plants, though some non-food plants like tropical mangrove also contain it. The other interesting thing about asparagusic acid is that it kills parasitic nematodes and protects the asparagus plant against them.

Some people cannot detect this characteristic smell and it was thought that genetically they did not produce the methyl mercaptan responsible for it. Recently, however, it is thought that all people excrete these smelly chemicals but that some people are unable to smell it. It has also been reported that other body fluids, notably semen, also bear the distinctive odour!

Other Properties

Asparagus contains no cholesterol, is very low in fat and sodium and is rich in vitamins A, E and C, folic acid, iron and potassium. It is also known as a natural remedy to help relieve indigestion and has been recommended as a mild sedative. It has diuretic properties, so the natives of Bretforton, near Evesham, eat it after boiling in saltwater with a sprig of mint and serve it with butter and buttered brown bread leaving them, presumably, with very clean kidneys! It is reported that green asparagus has ten times more vitamin A than white asparagus and almost twice as much iron.

One serving (5 spears or 93g) of green asparagus contains 20 calories, 0g fat, cholesterol or sodium, 5g total carbohydrates, 2g dietary fibre, 2g sugar, 2g protein, 10% RDA vitamin A, 10% RDA vitamin C, 2% RDA calcium, 2% RDA iron

'I leaned across the asparagus and asked her for a date'

JFK

Asparagus with Smoked Salmon and Poached Quails' Eggs

Ingredients

Serves 4 as a starter

16 spears of asparagus
**8 oz of smoked
salmon**
12 quails eggs
**2 tbs. of horseradish
sauce**
120g of caviar
Olive oil
**8 circles of toast 5cm
wide (white bread or
better still brioche)**

Stagg Inn, Titley, Kington,
Herefordshire, UK

Peel and trim asparagus to 4 cm lengths.
Cook until tender. Refresh in cold water.

Cut smoked salmon into 12 circles 5 cm
wide (use a pastry cutter).

Poach eggs in boiling water with a few
drops of white wine vinegar. Refresh in
cold water.

To assemble put a small dollop of
horseradish in the centre of each plate,
on top of that a smoked salmon round,
more horseradish then the toast circle,
repeat the layers until there are 3 layers
of smoked salmon and 2 layers of toast
on each plate. Re-heat the asparagus
and the quails' eggs in 2 pans of boiling
water. Roll the asparagus in olive oil to
give it a shine. Spoon the caviar around
the stack, arrange the asparagus on top
of the stack and put the quails eggs on
top of the caviar with black pepper and
salt sprinkled on the eggs.

Folklore

Every year in the Vale of Evesham an asparagus auction is held at the Fleece Inn in Bretforton. This famous pub, owned by the National Trust and maintained in its original condition, is in the heart of asparagus growing country. In fact several growers live very close by. An annual asparagus festival is now held centred on the auction and includes an asparagus festival day, asparagus quiz and asparagus gala ball in aid of local charities. The gala dinner features a three-course meal with... asparagus: from cream of asparagus soup to ham and local asparagus to asparagus ice cream (see page 85 for recipe) with shortbread and English strawberries. The festival is of course held in the middle of the season (in late May or early June).

A prize hundred

Local Traditions and Characters

Billy Byrd

One producer local to Bretforton is Billy Byrd, who described to me how gras is grown and recalled some of the traditions and folklore that surround it.

Billy met me in the barn opposite his vegetable stall and was joined by his brother to tell something of the traditions of gras. The season is only really six weeks long, he told me, from the end of April to mid-June. A good asparagus crown will need four or five buds at the end of the season to be useful the following year. They used to cultivate 17 acres in Bretforton and in those days a buyer named Poupart used to ship it all to London. For his trouble Poupart was treated to an expensive dinner at the Lygon Arms in nearby Broadway.

'You know, when you get your first asparagus, or your first acorn squash, or your first really good tomato of the season, those are the moments that define the cook's year. I get more excited by that than anything else.'

Mario Batali

Organic Trout with Asparagus, Roast Tomatoes, Herb Butter Sauce and Jersey Royals

Serves 4 as a main course
16 spears of asparagus
4 organic trout
2lb of jersey royals
or early potato
Rock salt
Olive oil
Balsamic vinegar
Salt and pepper
2-3 tbs. of chopped
mixed fresh herbs
(e.g. chives, chervil,
and tarragon)

....

For Beurre Blanc
100ml of dry
white wine
1 tbs. of white
wine vinegar
2 finely chopped
shallots
1 tbs. double cream
200g of cubed
unsalted butter
Salt

....

For roast tomatoes
8 tomatoes pref. plum
100ml of olive oil
Tarragon small bunch
Salt and pepper

....

Stagg Inn, Titley, Kington,
Herefordshire, UK

Scale and fillet the trout and remove the pin bones with tweezers. Rinse in cold water and dry (or ask your fishmonger to do this for you!)

For roast tomatoes: cut each tomato into eight, put all ingredients into a small baking tray and roast in a medium oven for 30 minutes. Liquidize with a stick blender then pass through a sieve.

Sprinkle the potatoes with rock salt, drizzle with olive oil and roast until lightly browned.

Peel and trim asparagus, then cook in boiling salted water until tender. Refresh in cold water.

To make beurre blanc, put wine, vinegar and shallots in a saucepan, bring to the boil and reduce by half. Add cream and bring to the boil. Lower the heat and gradually whisk in the cubes of butter. Season with salt and pepper to taste. Keep warm.

Heat some oil in a frying pan and cook the trout fillets for 45 seconds on each side.

Reheat asparagus in a frying pan with olive oil. Add a few drops of balsamic vinegar and remove from heat.

To assemble, put a small ladle of roast tomato sauce in the middle of the plate; place some new pots and asparagus spears on top. Lay trout fillets on top. Add freshly chopped herbs to the beurre blanc and pour around the plate.

The Fleece Inn, Bretforton, Worcestershire

Billy Byrd cont...

Billy used to have four acres and took a pitch at Birmingham market for 15 years. He found that it was a difficult market to get good prices, unlike London which bought up all that could be produced.

Billy's uncle visited the Evesham shoe shop run by Fred Robbins to buy shoes. Fred was paid in gras which was duly delivered during the season.

His Uncle Jack had tens of acres and always had cider in huge barrels. A quart of cider was allowed at the start of cutting a row of gras and a quart at the end of a row. One man fell off the dray after consuming more than his allowance.

The Byrd family have been in the village 700 years and have run the Fleece for 500 years. Many was the year that a raffle was held in the barn and the spears done up as half hundreds. Lola Taplin, who famously ran the pub in more recent times was Henry Byrd's great grandaughter.

Fred Archer - Splendour in the 'Gras'

Fred Archer, in his book *A Country Twelvemonth* tells of an asparagus cutting experience:

The account tells of Jubilee Day in May 1935 where Fred expected a goodday's holiday. However, the weather was hot and the gras had grown well. Ten cutters started out at first light and by 11.30 am the buds had been cut and taken to the 'gras-house' where women tied them into bundles with raffia. Harry Bailey, a partner of his father took four bundles at a timeand, with the help of a withy twig and a piece of webbing held tight with his foot, made the hundreds of asparagus. This 'hundreding up' was a specialist job and was followed by trimming the butt ends with a sharp knife. Nowadays the withies are no longer a crop on the banks of the nearby River Avon or found in the osier beds by the brooks. Hampers, made from withy twigs are now only to be found in the museum. On that May morning, it was 1 pm before the 'gras was loaded onto a dray and taken off to the train station to be sent to Nottingham. A hundred was sold for 12.5p.

Bretforton Silver Band

Bretforton gras is bound to another local institution, the Bretforton Silver Band. They play throughout the Asparagus Festival centred around the Fleece pub and many band members double up as auctioneer or help out at the festival.

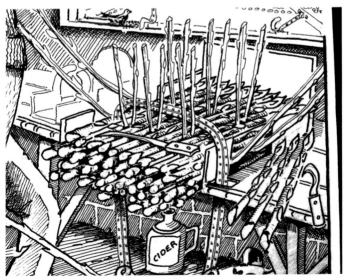

Hundreding up

Evelyn McKanan-Jones

Local artist Michael Barnard's aunt, Evelyn McKanan-Jones, wrote a poem running to 80 verses telling of her childhood during the 1900s. The following extract describes the gras season:

In the month of May, the asparagus grew

A crop that would wait for none

It meant work every day from the crack of dawn

'Til the season was over and done

They found time though to hold an Asparagus Show

An event they held with pride

Choosing the biggest and best of asparagus buds

They made bundles, at least a foot wide

And once a year, on a Sunday morn

The growers brought the best buds they could get

And together they made for charity

The biggest hundred yet

Outside our barn, a happy gathering then

As on hampers they sat in the sun

Sparing a few moments from their toil

Happy in work, well done

Tiring work, Michael Barnard

41

'Work! labour the asparagus me of life; the one great sacrament of humanity from which all other things flow - security, leisure, joy, art, literature, even divinity itself.'

Sean O'Casey

Asparagus and Goat's Cheese Tart

A puff pastry lined flan, baked with asparagus in a rich goat's cheese custard, served with balsamic vinegar dressed salad leaves.

SERVES 6
8 ozs / 250 gms of puff pastry (chilled or frozen)
1 bunch of spring onions
1 1/2 oz/50 gms butter
1 lb /450 gms asparagus
4 eggs
4 ozs / 100 gms of soft goat's cheese
6 fl oz / 200 ml milk
Salt & pepper
1 tbsp of chopped fresh tarragon

Evesham Hotel,
Evesham,
Worcestershire, UK

Roll out the puff pastry and line an 8in (20 cm) flan dish, brushed with a little oil first, and chill in a fridge for an hour if possible.

Wash and clean the spring onions and finely slice.

Place the butter in a saucepan and add the spring onions, season with a little salt and cook until soft.

Wash and trim the tough ends off the asparagus, remove the tips (approximately 2 ins or 5 cm long) and reserve. Cut the remainder into thin slices. Lightly cook the slices and the tips in boiling salted water for three minutes. Strain into a colander

In a food processor place the eggs and goats cheese and process until smooth. Add the milk and tarragon, season with salt and pepper.

Spread the sliced cooked spring onion and asparagus slices over the flan base and pour on the custard. Arrange the asparagus tips on top.

Bake in a moderate hot oven (200C) for 30/35 minutes.

Serve warm on a mixture of salad leaves tossed in balsamic vinegar.

Buster Mustoe and the Round of Gras

The former landlord of the Round of Gras, the only pub named after asparagus, was a well-known local character in Badsey and surrounding districts. He took over the Royal Oak, as the pub was previously known, in 1947 from his sister and 20 years later changed the name (see photo of the unveiling of the new pub sign in 1947). Asparagus dinners were simple affairs and Buster was always generous with the portions served. Since his retirement in 1987, the pub has changed hands a couple of times and has been run by Graham Brown for the last 6 years.

Graham has maintained the tradition of selling good local asparagus, simply. In the season the Round of Gras serves 800 asparagus meals per week. Over the time that the pub serves asparagus suppers, which runs from late April, until the 28th June (Graham's birthday), that would equal something like 2400 kg of gras! The most popular meal is asparagus with crispy bacon and parmesan shavings. Would Buster have approved? His trademark asparagus with thick-cut ham (often with the ham fat squeezed over the gras) lives on in the two main flavours and given the full tables during the season, locals and visitors alike approve.

The new sign at The Round of Gras

The pub is still full of asparagus artefacts from the pictures on the wall, the asparagus knives and two tine forks and now customers bring asparagus pottery in all shapes and sizes: jugs, plates and dishes are proudly displayed on a shelf over the carvery.

David Caswell

David Caswell is a third generation blacksmith who still makes asparagus knives. He tells many asparagus related stories about harvesting and eating this delectable vegetable. On the badsey.net website is a photo dated 1927 of his father and grandfather and David hopes to be able to celebrate the Caswell's centenary in 2009. At his parents' wedding in the third week of April, it was so warm that it was all his father could do to cut the day's crop before sprinting to the wedding service.

The Forge, Badsey

'I revere the memory of Mr. F. as an estimable man and most indulgent husband, only necessary to mention Asparagus and it appeared or to hint at any little delicate thing to drink and it came like magic in a pint bottle; it was not ecstasy but it was comfort.'

Charles Dickens

Cold Sauces for Asparagus

Jane Grigson's Good Things

Jane Grigson

ISBN 0-141469-013

1971

Published by Michael
Joseph/Penguin

Vinaigrette aux fines herbes

1 tablespoon lemon juice, or tarragon wine vinegar, beaten up with salt, pepper, a teaspoon of sugar, and 5—6 tablespoons of olive oil. Flavour with plenty of chopped parsley, tarragon, chervil, and chives or spring onion tops.

Mayonnaise Maltese style

2 egg yolks, salt, pepper. well beaten together with 1 teaspoon lemon juice or wine vinegar. Drop by drop, beat in ¼ pint olive oil; then another ¼ pint in a steady stream. Season with more lemon juice or vinegars and the grated rind and juice of a blood orange.

Tarragon Cream

Tarragon cream (a delicious, quickly-made sauce from Food for the Greedy Nancy Shaw, published in 1936 by Cobden-Sanderson):

Season some thick cream with salt and pepper and a dust of curry powder; and whip it until thick. Then flavour it by adding gradually a few drops of white tarragon vinegar and place it on ice for a short time before being served. To be sent up in a sauce boat for cold asparagus. Don't overdo the chilling: in the thirties, domestic refrigerators were the new kitchen toy, food was chilled whenever possible — not always a good thing for delicate flavours.

Dijon Sauce

Crush the yolk of a hard-boiled egg with 3 petits suisses cheeses, to a smooth paste. Add 2 tablespoons Dijon mustard, then drop by drop 4 oz. oil. Flavour with lemon juice. It should be the consistency of mayonnaise.

'After 20 annual visits, I am still surprised each time I return to see this giant asparagus bed of alabaster and rose and green skyscrapers.'

Cecil Beaton

Grilled John Dory Asparagus and Saffron Lasagne with Bay Leaf, Pistachio and Pink Grapefruit

SERVES 4
4 100g fillets
John Dory
Olive oil for cooking
Salt and pepper
12 spears of
asparagus, peeled
and left whole

FOR SAFFRON PASTA
290g pasta flour
1/2 tsp salt
2 whole eggs
3 egg yolks
5 ml olive oil
1 tsp saffron

FOR BAY LEAF SAUCE
Oil for cooking
I chopped shallot
200 ml dry white wine
400 ml fish stock
100 ml double cream
4 bay leaves
salt and white pepper

FOR PISTACHIO AND PINK GRAPEFRUIT DRESSING
100g of salted
pistachios, out
of their shell
1 pink grapefruit,
segmented and cut
into 1 cm pieces
100 ml olive oil
Salt and pepper

Recipe created by Nathan
Outlaw, head chef at St
Ervan Manor, Padstow,
Cornwall, UK

Oil and season the fillets of John Dory and place on a grill tray. In a large pan of simmering salted water cook the asparagus for one minute and refresh in ice water, then drain. Refrigerate fish and asparagus until needed.

Pasta: mix all the ingredients together by hand until a dough forms. Knead dough for one minute, cling film and rest at room temperature for 30 minutes. Roll the dough through a pasta machine, folding in half each time until it becomes smooth and elastic. Roll to the thinnest setting and cut into squares. Bring a large pan of salted water to the simmer and blanch the pasta for 1 minute. Refresh in ice cold water and drain onto a tea towel. Store in a container with some oil to stop it sticking. Three squares per portion will be enough.

Bay leaf sauce: in a pan add a little oil and the shallot and bay leaves. Sweat for 1 minute and add the wine. Reduce by half. Then add the fish stock and reduce again. Finally, add the double cream and simmer for 2 minutes, season to taste and strain through a sieve. Cool and refrigerate until needed.

Dressing: in a food processor add the oil and half of the pistachios and blitz until smooth. Pour into a bowl and add the remaining pistachios, grapefruit and seasoning. Retain until ready to serve.

For completion of the dish, pre heat the grill. Place the fish under the grill and cook for approx 4-5 minutes. While the fish are cooking, heat the bay leaf sauce and add the asparagus and the pasta. Cook for one minute and remove from the heat. Arrange the asparagus and pasta in the centre of four hot bowls. Add the bay leaf sauce and lay the fish on top. Finally spoon on the dressing and serve.

Blowing our own trumpet

In selling we excel

Trade Mark

Cultivation and Markets

Where does asparagus grow? There are about 300 species of asparagus growing in Asia, Africa, Europe and the Americas. Many are climbing plants with edible young stems. It is often seen around southern Europe and grows in sandy soils near coasts and in volcanic regions. It is also seen in Russia where wild asparagus is eaten by cattle and horses.

In the British Isles, wild asparagus is commonest in sandy places by the sea and on cliffs. For example, near the Lizard peninsula in Cornwall and in Angelsea in Wales. Asparagus Island off the Lizard is named after the wild asparagus growing there.

Asparagus can be forced, i.e. grown under artificial conditions and in England these crops can be cut as early as mid-March. In an attempt to raise the profile of the vegetable, an asparagus run was held for the early season crop in April 2002. The first rounds were whisked in a Morgan motor car (still manufactured in nearby Malvern) to the Savoy Hotel in London where waiting journalists were treated to an asparagus lunch.

Purists, however, insist on waiting for naturally grown asparagus. Nigel Smith, landlord of The Fleece pub in Bretforton, Worcestershire, the site of the annual asparagus auction, says 'If you want really good asparagus, you should wait until the weather is warmer and the natural stuff starts coming up'.

Evesham Growers

There are many growers in the Evesham area. Paul Haden at First Gras in Pershore (where they began the first local growing under glass in 1992), Billy Byrd at Bretforton, Nick Coley in Harvington, Patrick Brotherton in Badsey, Bob Hall

In the asparagus field

in Offenham, George Keen, Brian Jelfs and Mr Aldchurch in Badsey.

Michael Barnard, the local artist, lives in Badsey and his family used to keep 40 acres under cultivation. He tells of the tradition of a post-harvest session where an 80-gallon barrel of cider was drunk by the men who each brought their choicest buds (at least 13 inches long) to show off. They were eventually rescued by their womenfolk!

In the period before the war, the main areas of cultivation in the Evesham area were Badsey and Bretforton as well as near Hinton-on-the-Green, where Newman's were the main grower in the clay soils there.

Today, Billy Byrd farms just one acre, still cut by hand. Each spear is cut with a purpose-designed knife and an acre typically yields 60 rounds. Each day the cutting must be done and typically takes an hour for the experienced grower.

Others in the area such as W R Haines harvest by mechanical means. Many mechanical harvesters have been devised and patented and rely on a complex series of wheels, discs, wires and other paraphernalia to co-ordinate the equipment amongst the rows, find and position the bud and cut it and store it, all without harming the delicate crop.

Presentation

Asparagus has long been a prime crop of market gardeners in the Vale of Evesham. The delicious buds of the plant are harvested for a short period only during May and June and great pride is taken in its presentation: a small bundle, or round, will these days weigh a pound or perhaps a kilo; the large 'hundred', which perversely contains 120 buds, is of specially selected buds and is held together by woven withy (willow twigs). The preparation of the hundred is a craft in itself.

Billy Byrd learned from his father how to tie the hundreds.

'You start by taking willow twigs, known locally as withy twigs, which are stuck into the ground and allowed to grow to two feet tall in osier beds. The side twigs are cut in December when the sap is down. They are bundled up and rolled in Hessian and buried. When dug up they are more pliable. Raffia (raffy) is used and 200-300 hundreds might be prepared.'

Gras was also sent out as flats (the transport boxes) in bundles and in wicker baskets.

A bundle comprised 15 buds tied with raffia and known as a score. Eight scores tied together made a hundred (containing 120 buds).

Bundles with 30 buds became more common after the war.

'Do it quicker than you can cook asparagus' *(Citius quam asparagi coquentur)*

Augustus

Marinated Asparagus

SERVES 3-4
900 g/2 lb asparagus
Coarse-grain sea salt
Juice of 1 large lemon
4 shallots, finely
chopped
1 teaspoon of
dried rigani (Greek
oregano)
1 small bunch of flat
leaf parsley, leaves
coarsely chopped
1 teaspoon cracked
black pepper
175 ml/6 fl oz
extra virgin olive
oil, or to taste

Flavours of Greece
Rosemary Barron
ISBN 1-902304-28 4
2000
Published by Grubb Street
London

This superbly flavoured seasonal dish requires little work but it does demand top-quality ingredients: tender young asparagus with a fresh bright colour; a good fruity olive oil, and the juice of a plump fresh lemon. Choose asparagus of a similar thickness for even cooking. The dish can be prepared several hours ahead – the longer the asparagus rests in the marinade, the more mellow the flavour. Serve plenty of crusty bread for your guests to mop up the sauce.

Break off the tough ends of the asparagus at the point where they snap easily and discard. Add 5 cm/2 inches of water and salt to taste to a shallow saucepan large enough to hold the asparagus in a double layer. Bring to the boil and add the asparagus. Simmer for 3-5 minutes, or until barely tender, drain, and spread on paper towels to dry. (Or steam the asparagus.)

Whisk together the lemon juice, shallots, rigani, parsley, pepper and salt to taste, and olive oil in a large shallow bowl. Add the asparagus and toss gently to coat. Cover and set aside at room temperature for up to 1 hour or refrigerate for up to 4 hours, but remove from the refrigerator 15 minutes before serving.

To serve, carefully toss the asparagus with the marinade once more and transfer to a platter. Season to taste with salt and pepper and serve.

Farm shop in Hampton, Evesham

The growing cycle

Seed is planted in the spring of the first year in a nursery bed. One year later the seedling roots or crowns are planted in permanent beds. Crowns are spaced 15 inches (38 cm) apart and covered in each row 3.5 feet (1.1 m) apart.

For the next two years the plants are left to develop. Buds are not cut but kept weed free. Other crops used to be planted between the growing buds.

Ridging the beds

Bower or fern were cut off in October or by Bonfire Night (5th November) at the latest.

Then bedding out is done with forkfuls of soil carefully banked around the plant. The soil is bed-forked and this can be done mechanically. Older stalks known as kecks are knocked off and burnt. More soil is then drawn up (bed-moulding). The fourth season is the first harvest, so that the root system is well developed and strong.

Fred Archer, writing in *Warwickshire and Worcestershire Life* in 1985, described the ways he used to cultivate asparagus:

'They used a bouting-out plough to create the furrows nine inches deep. After planting the crowns, they were carefully covered with soil thrown up by the plough's 'scratters'. This is a four-prong fork with narrow tines at right angles and is a term peculiar to Evesham.'

Commercial growers reckon asparagus crowns have a life of between three to ten years with the middle years being the most productive, although crowns have been known to last 100 years.

Asparagus varieties

Locally around Evesham, larger producers such as Haines or Bomfords use F1 hybrid gras to produce uniform and vigorous crop from seed, while smaller growers use the open pollinated type of asparagus.

The hybrid has a better yield and bigger bud. However, big does not always taste the best. Many cooks shave off the green outer layer but Billy Byrd and his brother believe that is where all the flavour is. His brother usually took the 'sprue' home for his wife to cook, but one week he was offered some special gras (the so-called premium crop with larger buds) and took them home for his supper. After the meal his wife asked him not to bring that gras home again as it was not as tasty as the usual sprue in all its bent and twisted shapes! The categories of asparagus range from special, best and sprue, the latter being the fine buds.

Nineteenth-century varieties included 'Connover's Colossal', 'Argenteuil' and Sutton's 'Giant'. Other varieties are selected to thrive in heavy clay soil, typical of the Evesham

Asparagus is best prepared simply

area ('Giant Mammoth'), or to be all-male ('Saxon') or to be tolerant of disease. High yield varieties such as 'Gijnlim' can produce 12 spears per plant.

In the USA, asparagus comes in the following grades: colossal, jumbo, large, standard and small. Varieties are interchangeable in recipes, with the only change being in the colour of the resultant dish.

White asparagus can be produced from any variety by the exclusion of light. Soil is mounded over the plants to keep them in the dark and darkness must be maintained throughout harvesting, which makes this type expensive.

Asparagus grows wild in some areas, particularly in Europe but is rarely seen in markets except perhaps in southern Europe.

Taste

Can different varieties or locations be distinguished by different tastes? As far as we can tell, although a blind tasting has never been done, taste is not uniquely identified with location.

Market gardening woman, with a handful of asparagus.

'Ambassadors cropped up like hay, Prime Ministers and such as they grew like asparagus in May, and dukes were three a penny.'
William Gilbert

'I try to get them working. My older son is 10 and he's pretty interested. We had a dinner party the other night and he helped a lot. He helped peel asparagus; he hung out. It was great.'

Todd English

Asparagus with Polonaise Sauce

SERVES 4

**2 bundles fresh
asparagus (about
500g or 1 lb)
Salt and pepper
to taste
2 hard-boiled eggs
60 g (2 oz) butter
4 tablespoons fresh
breadcrumbs**

Charmain Solomen's
Complete Vegetarian
Cookbook
Charmain Solomen
2000
Published by HarperCollins
ISBN 1 902 304 28 4

Prepare the asparagus, snapping off tough ends of stems and peeling the bottom half of the stalks. Wash well. Sometimes there is fine sand lurking in the tips.

In a pan large enough to accommodate the spears lying down, bring to the boil enough lightly salted water to cover the asparagus. Drop in the spears and cover the pan to bring back to the boil quickly, then uncover and simmer until just tender.

Drain well, season to taste, then serve sprinkled with finely chopped hard-boiled eggs (some prefer just the yolk, pushed through a sieve). Heat the butter until nut brown, then quickly fry the breadcrumbs and sprinkle over the asparagus.

Flemish Asparagus

**2 lbs asparagus
3 hard-boiled eggs
4 oz melted butter
salt and pepper**

Author unknown
World Cookery
1962
Published by The National
Magazine Company,
Morrison and Gibb Ltd

Trim 2 lb of asparagus and cut it into even-sized lengths. Wash it very thoroughly, then plunge it into slightly salted boiling water and cook for 12-15 minutes. Prepare a sauce: sieve the yolks of 3 hard-boiled eggs, add 4 oz melted butter gradually and season with salt and pepper. Serve with the sauce poured over the asparagus.

Authors note: Reduce cooking time to avoid overcooking.

'Ambassadors cropped up like hay, Prime Ministers and such as they grew like asparagus in May, and dukes were three a penny.'

William Gilbert

Butter Roast Sand Hutton Asparagus with Aged York Ham, Fried Village Quail Egg, Bubble & Squeak, Grain Mustard Velouté

4 spears of pared and blanched asparagus
1 Slice of York ham
Seasoning
Clarified butter
4 x 6cm bubble & squeak potato cakes (Savoy cabbage and smoked bacon)
4 x quail eggs

Velouté
1 teaspoon grain mustard
A splash of white wine
A splash of whipping cream
Reduce all by half and check seasoning

Star Inn, Harome,
North Yorkshire, UK

Chef's note

This dish is on our menu at the moment and has proved very popular having sold c.200lb of Asparagus and ½ stone of York Ham in the past two weeks!

To me, this is what regional cuisine is all about, village quail eggs from Marwood's farm 50 yards away, local asparagus and aged York Ham from Andrew Radford of Radford's Butchers at Sleights, nr Whitby (01947 810229), whom I have known from childhood as I lived in the village.

Andrew Radford uses "Old English White" female highbred gilts which have a little more fat than usual to provide moisture. The leg is part boned by removing the hip bone, the hock shaped and then dried in tubs for 3–4 weeks in a brown sugar and saltpetre cure. After this the ham is rinsed, then wrapped in paper and net and hung for 1–3 years.

Method

Tightly wrap four spears of asparagus in York ham and season.

Warm a little clarified butter, gently roast the asparagus in a shallow frying pan for 1–2 minutes, add the floured potato cakes. When they are lightly coloured flip them over and place the pan in a moderate oven for a further 2–3 minutes.

Gently fry the quails eggs whilst the asparagus is coming through.

Asparagus sale at Smithfield Market

Season

In the Northern hemisphere, the traditional asparagus season lasts between 1st May and 21st June or later in, for example, Germany. These dates are controversial and many opinions exist. Some say that harvesting after the 14th or 15th June is not advised as the buds go pale. The first season for a plant may end early (19th June) and often in warm weather there are two cuts per day, the first cut starting early around dawn.

In the Southern hemisphere the season is reversed with crops being cut in October onwards. Peru growers have extended the growing cycle to a year-round crop by using different altitudes and locations.

Asparagus in Europe and elsewhere

In Spain, the asparagus sector in the Extremadura region wants Protected Denomination of Origin. The production in

Extremadura comes early in the season and producers want to differentiate the quality of their fresh product more distinctively from produce from Navarra and imported brands. In Spain many companies supply the processing industry, but an increasing number of them have successfully exported fresh quality produce.

Schrobenhausen Asparagus Museum

Well-known in Italy is white asparagus from Cantello, Lombardy, where asparagus cultivation began in the 1930s. This production was highly appreciated until the 1960s, but by then the asparagus from Cantello was at risk of dying out due to changing tastes. A fair takes place in Cantello each year, on the second Sunday of May, in order to celebrate the end of the asparagus harvest.

In France, asparagus was notably grown around Paris (the Argenteuil district) and in the Loire valley. It is also grown in Provence, where it is often protected by wind breaks.

In Germany, May is asparagus month and many restaurants display 'spargelkartes' (asparagus menus) with everything from soups and salads to main dishes and deserts all featuring asparagus. In Berlin, the TV Tower (Fernsehturm) on Alexanderplatz, Berlin-Mitte has the local nickname of 'Asparagus Tower' because of its shape. Berliners consider the white asparagus with its

subtle, delicate flavour the more refined product. The tradition stems back to the 17th century, when French Huguenots brought green asparagus to the region. The Schlunkendorf Museum close to the sandy fields of Beelitz, south of Berlin is entirely devoted to asparagus and features exhibits on botany, cultivation and culinary presentation. There is also a museum in Bavaria (Schrobenhausen).

Huge quantities are grown in California in the USA, where the annual asparagus festival in Stockton is justifiably famous.

Year-round supplies are available from the biggest grower, Peru.

Japan is the largest net importer of asparagus.

'Are you casting asparagus on my cooking?'

Curly Howard

Asparagus and Almonds in Filo

5 oz (140 g) butter
1 onion, peeled and
finely chopped
1lb (455 g) asparagus,
trimmed and blanched
4 oz (110 g) flaked
almonds, toasted
6 tbsp single cream
4 oz (110g) Cheddar
cheese, grated
Salt
Freshly ground
black pepper
5 sheets Filo pastry

Times Cookbook
Frances Bissell
1993
Chatto and Windus
ISBN 0 701145 439

Make the filling first. Melt 1 oz (30 g) of the butter and fry the onion until softened. Cut the asparagus into 1 in (2.5 cm) pieces, and fry briefly with the onion without letting it colour. Remove the pan from the heat, and stir in the almonds, cream and cheese. Season to taste, and cool. Meanwhile, melt the remaining butter and preheat the oven to 200˚ C/400˚ F/Mark 6. Lay one sheet of Filo pastry on a work surface. Cover the remaining sheets with a clean, damp cloth. Brush the first sheet with melted butter and cover with a second. Brush again with melted butter and repeat with the remaining three sheets. Spread the asparagus filling over the pastry, leaving a 1 in/2.5 cm border around the edge. Fold in the two shorter sides and then roll up. Carefully brush with the remaining butter and bake in the oven for 20 minutes. Turn the oven down to 180˚ C/350˚ F/Mark 4, and cook for a further 10 minutes until crisp and golden brown.

*The asparagus china display at the
Round of Gras pub in Badsey*

Markets and the popularity of asparagus

The marketing of asparagus to local farmers' markets, farm shops and road-side stalls is still a fiercely competitive business. Gary Andrews who cultivates asparagus in the centre of Evesham, in the shadow of Evesham Bell Tower, has planted extensively and prices have fallen to £1.50 a round. Backed by heavy radio advertising he is causing concern among the traditional farmers who expect £3-£5 a round depending on the time of the season and the weather.

Harvesting

Asparagus spears can be cut or snapped when they are 6 to 10 inches tall. Gras is cut first thing in the morning because it keeps better in the shade and the buds are cooler and more easily snapped-off, which also improves quality. The snapping method is faster and less expensive than cutting. Cutting at or below the soil surface with a long-handled asparagus knife is a skilled task. The gras bud is held firmly and the knife pushed into the ground at about 45 degrees until it comes up against the plant stem. One cut releases the bud, which will be white at the base where light has not penetrated.

Gras can grow many inches in one day (some say they can see it grow) and for large commercial growers timing is everything. A cutting team may leave a field that is not ready only to return later that day to a crop that is 'blown' and useless.

Asparagus is cut (or snapped off) rather than being picked since it is still connected to its root or crown. Nowadays most asparagus is grown in flat fields rather than the traditional raised beds.

Tools

To harvest from the often muddy raised beds, an asparagus knife was developed. The only remaining producer, David Caswell of Badsey Forge in Worcestershire, took great care and pleasure in explaining how these knives are made and used:

Some 14 inches (36 cm) long the knives have three flattened teeth, set at an angle and sharpened. Made of tempered steel they are used by pushing into the mounded soil to sever the base of the spear. Older knives had four notches but the three teeth are more common. Nowadays, asparagus knives, though still prized by individual growers, are something of a curiosity.

To help with the cultivation, a two-tine Evesham clay fork was used. It is said that the clay soils, common in the Vale of Evesham, are part of the secret behind Evesham's fame as an asparagus growing area. These forks were developed to help turn the heavy, sticky soil and having just two prongs made them easier to handle. Nowadays many growers do not earth up the furrows at all.

Modern-day cutting uses machines specially adapted for the task. These machines have exercised inventors, since cutting the crop with accuracy and avoiding wastage is tricky. Most available harvesters are non-selective and reduce yield 35 to 50% in comparison to hand cutting. Around 30 to 40 acres of asparagus are required to justify most harvesting machines and the cleaning equipment needed to clean machine-harvested asparagus before packing and marketing.

Traditional Evesham asparagus knife

Enjoying cider in the packing shed, Michael Barnard

Processing and Storage

Fresh asparagus is highly perishable and deteriorates rapidly at high temperatures. For commercial growers the crop has to be cooled to remove the 'field heat'.

Processing may include washing, trimming and packing. The demand for fine sprue and tips for stir-frying mean that the unused parts end up in upmarket soups.

Canned asparagus is produced in great quantities in the US and often ends up in welfare food programs. While many recipes exist for it, its use in catering is mainly decorative and given the year-round availability of fresh asparagus it is of limited interest to the asparagus aficionado.

Asparagus may be frozen and it is said that this retains nutrients better than the canning process. Asparagus can be sun dried but when reconstituted can be brownish and has the texture of canned asparagus. Preserved asparagus comes in many forms such as pastes, purees, pickles and chutneys. In China, asparagus spears are candied and served as special treats.

Asparagus

Mr. Ramsbottom went to the races,
A thing as he'd ne'er done before,
And as luck always follers beginners,
Won five pounds, no-less and no-more.

He felt himself suddenly tempted
To indulge in some reckless orgee,
So he went to a caffy-a-teerer
And had a dressed crab with his tea.

He were crunching the claws at the finish
And wondering what next he would do,
Then his thoughts turned to home and
to Mother,
And what she would say when she knew.

For Mother were dead against racing
And said as she thought 'twere a sin
For people to gamble their money
Unless they were certain to win.

These homely domestic reflections
Seemed to cast quite a gloom on Pa's day
He thought he'd best take home a
present
And square up the matter that way.

'Twere a bit ofa job to decide on
What best to select for this 'ere,
So he started to look in shop winders
In hopes as he'd get some idea.

He saw some strange stuff in a fruit shop
Like leeks with their nobby ends gone,
It were done up in bundles like firewood-
Said Pa to the Shopman, "What's yon?"

"That's Ass-paragus-what the Toffs eat"
Were the answer; said Pa "That 'll suit,
I'd best take a couple of bundles,
For Mother's a bobby for fruit."

He started off home with his purchase
And pictured Ma all the next week
Eating sparagus fried with her bacon
Or mashed up in bubble-and-squeak.

He knew when she heard he'd been
racing
She'd very nigh talk him to death,
So he thought as he'd call in the ' Local'
To strengthen his nerve and his breath.

He had hardly got up to the counter
When a friend of his walked in the bar,
He said "What ye got in the bundle?"
"A present for Mother," said Pa.

It's 'sparagus stuff what the Toffs eat "
His friend said "It's a rum-looking plant,
Can I have the green ends for my
rabbits?"
said Pa "Aye, cut off what you want.

He cut all the tips off one bundle,
Then some more friends arrived one
by one,
And all of them seemed to keep rabbits
Pa had no green ends left when they'd
done.

When he got home the 'ouse were in
dark ness,
So he slipped in as sly as a fox,
Laid the 'sparagus on kitchen table
And crept up to bed in his socks.

He got in without waking Mother,
A truly remarkable feat,
And pictured her telling the neighbours
As 'twere 'sparagus-what the toffs eat.

But when he woke up in the morning
It were nigh on a quarter to ten,
There were no signs of Mother, or
breakfast
Said Pa, "What's she done with her-sen?"

He shouted "What's up theer in t'
kitchen?"
She replied, "You do well to enquire,
Them bundles of chips as you brought
home
Is so damp... I can't light the fire."

Marriott Edgar (1880 - 1951)

Bacon and Asparagus Fraze

2 eggs
1 ounce flour
scant 1/4 pint
single cream
salt and white pepper
3 ounces onion
3 ounces cooked
ham or bacon
asparagus tips (cook
fresh asparagus
or use tinned)
butter for frying

Fine English Cookery
Michael Smith
1973
Published by Faber
ISBN 0 571 111 28 9,

The fraze has completely disappeared from our repertoire, for what reason I cannot imagine, as this omelette-cum-pancake is a very tasty first course or a main course for lunch or high tea

Make a batter with the eggs, flour and cream, season, and add a little water if it is too thick. Finely slice the onion and the bacon or ham. Fry these in butter until golden brown. Drain the fat away. Drain the asparagus tips if using tinned. Make up small pancakes from the batter, adding a mixture of the onion, ham and asparagus tips before turning the fraze over to brown on the second side. Serve as quickly as possible after cooking.

Just how many you make will depend on the generosity of the filling and the size of fraze you like to serve, but each fraze should have an abundant filling. I count on the above quantities to make four.

Growers Associations and Shows

The Vale of Evesham Horticultural Society was established in March 1827 but no longer exists. Many other older societies, which presented prizes and maintained quality have also long since disappeared. The Badsey show was taken over by The Vale of Evesham Asparagus Growers Association. The Vale of Evesham Asparagus Association, formed in 1924, held an annual show at the Royal Oak (later known as the Round of Gras) where its charismatic landlord Buster Mustoe cooked asparagus suppers. These shows finished in 1976.

In 1919, 70 entries were made in a show held on 28th May with £16 prize money. £196 was made in total and £21 was paid for the best hundred (£3 per bud in today's money).

Grading schemes for gras were introduced in the 1920s and special paper wrappers produced, a far cry from the use of elastic bands nowadays. One short-term policy of the growers' society that was quickly changed was that of paying for any loss – during a glut, poor quality produce together with good asparagus, was sent in the knowledge that growers would be paid for all they produced. This policy was soon stopped.

SUPER ASPARAGUS
LEGION'S FINE EFFORT

This bundle of asparagus was sold in Covent Garden Market in 1937. The £5 6s. raised contributed to the building of the British Legion Hall in Badsey.

In the UK the Asparagus Growers Association holds special events days for growers and marketers of the vegetable.

Other Crops that Take the Name of Asparagus

Asparagus lettuce is a type of lettuce not asparagus. Also known as 'Cracoviensis' or stem lettuce, it is a very old lettuce variety described by Vilmorin-Andrieux at the end of the 19th century.

The asparagus pea (*Tetragonolobus purpurea*) has pods which taste like asparagus and are best cooked and served like gras itself.

The asparagus bean (*Vigna sesquipedalis*), also known as the yard-long bean, grows in warmer climates and produces beans that can be up to a metre in length.

The future of asparagus

The popularity of asparagus will continue to increase dramatically in the UK, fuelled by a number of factors. People are motivated these days by the desire for local fresh produce, the Slow Food Movement or saving air miles and this is combined with a wider availability of the crop at more attractive prices. More fields will be put under cultivation because neither the small local growers or larger commercials with 300 or more acres under cultivation can meet the demand.

Will mass production and prices as low as that paid for cabbage destroy the specialness of gras? Hopefully not. When all the hype is stripped away, this is still a unique, tasty and attractive vegetable that makes any meal great.

There are many who share the passion for asparagus. Although many of the market gardeners in the Vale of Evesham are no longer with us, there is a new generation of growers. Organic methods, forced under glass or on a large scale for supermarket consumption – all of these represent the new face for this passion which continues unabated.

'The whole vegetable tribe have lost their gust with me. Only I stick to asparagus, which still seems to inspire gentle thoughts.'

Charles Lamb

The Asparagus and The Italian!

Sarah Poli of Firenze
Restaurant,
9 Station Street
Kibworth Beauchamp,
Leicestershire, UK

A little while after my husband and I set up home, he cooked for me a dish that has gone on to serve many in our restaurant ever since.

My husband is a chef, so I should have had more faith when I questioned,

'What on earth are you up to with that asparagus?'

It all started safely enough! Simply steamed, beautiful, vibrant, fresh, *in season* asparagus. Even the sizzling butter and Parmesan looked safe enough... but then an egg, not to say, a fried egg!

Amazing! Quite simply to die for! And so say all that have been presented with it since.

The dish is simplicity itself.

A few steamed stems of asparagus, laid hot on a plate sprinkled with fresh grated parmesan, a fried egg on top, and then nut brown butter poured over the lot.... Awesome!

For the faint hearted, you can serve it without the egg, and simply with Parmesan and butter.

The Preparation and Eating of Asparagus

Asparagus is best eaten fresh, which means within a few hours of being harvested. And whether your preference is for thick or thin, green or purple, choose freshly cut gras which retains its spring.

After washing, a variety of advice exists about how to prepare the spears and cook the asparagus.

Some say you should snap the spear and it will break at a point above the woody and tough lower portion.

Others advocate cutting off all of the white portion and then using a vegetable peeler to remove the tough skin. The trimmings can be used to flavour stock for example for risottos or added to the cooking water to reduce the amount of taste and vitamins lost during the cooking process.

Asparagus may be boiled, steamed, fried or even griddled! Evesham locals insist on a sprig of mint in the cooking water in the same way that new potatoes or peas are sometimes cooked.

The use of asparagus steamers to protect the delicate buds while ensuring the spears are properly cooked is more useful as a fashion accessory. In the hands of a reasonably competent cook the delicate buds can be lightly steamed if left exposed above boiling water.

While elaborate recipes exist, particularly for the not-recommended tinned variety, the simplest treatment is for melted butter to be poured over the steaming spears, perhaps with some fresh crusty bread.

Locals speak of cooking some boiled gammon, asparagus and new potatoes and squeezing some fat from the cooked gammon over the steaming spears.

Cooking spears *al dente* is a mistake. As with French beans any toughness or squeakiness means they are underdone. The spear should droop slightly when held by the stem (white) end.

John Jenkinson tells of a diner who proceeded to eat asparagus stalk first, in other words upside down:

'A middle-aged couple ordered plain asparagus with butter. The waitress brought them to the table in a pretty full restaurant. They held the bud and started eating at the stem end. The weird thing was that word somehow got round the restaurant and virtually everyone was surreptitiously looking at them and smirking but the couple appeared not to notice. Needless to say the plates took longer to clear this way than in the traditional manner(!) and I'll never know how the waitress kept a straight face as she cleared away the two neat plates of the perfect, soft asparagus buds!! The asparagus was pronounced excellent.'

And this has been repeated several times at the Round of Gras Pub as well with the delicate tips being left as waste.

A local Badsey man took some bundles up to a hotel in Yorkshire many years ago. They were unfamiliar with its preparation and cut off and threw away the tips and proceeded to cook the rest!

Asparagus in steamer basket

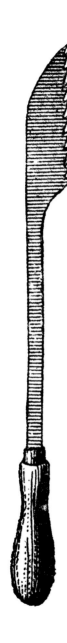

The Wonderful and Not So Wonderful World of Asparagus Recipes

Some books give methods and recipes for:

- Asparagus puree - and use in the making of pasta or noodles
- Asparagus juice
- Asparagus stock
- Raw asparagus used as in crudités
- Marinated raw asparagus (see recipe, page 55)
- Pickled asparagus
- Asparagus vinaigrette
- Spreads and toasties made with asparagus puree and cheese
- Breads and patties
- Sauces for simple boiled asparagus
- Butter
- Various herb, nut and citrus butters
- Mayonnaise, plain and flavoured
- Classic sauces such as vinaigrette, Hollandaise etc.
- Cream, plain and flavoured

Bizarre recipes include:

- Asparagus in avocado boats
- Curried asparagus and chicken livers
- Asparagus custard puffs

Old engraving of asparagus knife

'Pray how does your asparagus perform?'

John Adams, in a letter to his wife Abigail

Petits Crèmes d'Asperges Sauce Maltaise

Little asparagus creams with Maltaise sauce

SERVES 6

CREAMS
1.5 kg (3½ lbs)
asparagus, peeled,
trimmed and washed
Salt
300 ml (1/2 pint)
double cream, heated
6 egg yolks, beaten
Salt and freshly
ground white pepper
Freshly grated
nutmeg
6 lettuce leaves
and 6 sprigs of
coriander or parsley

SAUCE
2 tablespoons
white wine
2 tablespoons white
wine vinegar
6 peppercorns
Half a bay leaf
Juice of half
an orange
3 egg yolks beaten
125g (4 oz) unsalted
butter, melted
1 teaspoon cold water
Grated zest of
an orange
Salt

Restaurant Dishes of the World
Margaret Fulton
1983
Published by Octopus
ISBN 0 760 419 40 5

To make the creams: remove the coarse ends and cut off the tips of the asparagus about 1 cm (1/2 inch) below the head. Reserve the tips. Place trimmed stalks in a steamer set over boiling water, sprinkle with salt, and steam for 30 minutes. Puree stalks in a blender or food processor fitted with the steel blade.

Combine the asparagus puree, heated cream and egg yolks and season to taste with salt, pepper and nutmeg. Butter 6 small soufflé dishes (approximately 150ml/ 1/4 pint capacity). Divide the asparagus mixture among them. Place the dishes in a large baking dish and add enough hot water to come half-way up their sides. Bake in a preheated moderate oven (180 C/350 F/Gas 4) for 25-35 minutes or until the creams are set.

After the creams go into the oven, bring a small saucepan of salted water to the boil and cook reserved asparagus tips until tender, about 4 minutes. Drain and set aside. When the creams are cooked, remove them from the oven and allow them to rest for 10 minutes.

While the creams are resting prepare the sauce. Place wine, vinegar, peppercorns and bay leaf in a saucepan and boil over high heat until reduced to 1 tablespoon. Add orange juice and drain into the basin containing the beaten egg yolks. Place the basin over a pan of simmering water (do not let the bottom of the basin touch the water) and beat with a whisk until frothy and beginning to thicken. Gradually add the melted butter beating continuously (as sauce thickens, add more butter, beating until all is used). Remove from heat, beat in the cold water and add the orange zest. Stir in salt to taste.

Arrange a lettuce leaf on each of 6 heated plates (preferably white) and unmould a cream, coat with hot sauce and garnish each plate with a sprig of coriander or parsley.

Glossary of Terms

Bower	Same as fern
Bud	A single asparagus stem
Crown	The root system
Fern	The flowery stems appearing in Autumn
Flat	A hamper or box designed for transporting rounds
Gras	Asparagus
Half-hundred	4 rounds totalling 56 buds
Hundred	8 rounds totalling 120 buds
Kecks	The decayed stem remnants cleared during the Autumn
Ozier Bed	Willow twig bed used to tie rounds
Raffy	Raffia, a type of string
Round	A number of buds usually governed by weight
Sparrow-grass	Asparagus
Spear	A bud or stem
Sprue (or Sprew)	Fine or thin asparagus of good flavour but not seen as attractive
Withy twigs	Willow twigs used for tying rounds
Asum gras	Evesham asparagus

Asparagus Ice Cream

1½ pints milk
12 egg yolks
200g sugar
½ pint cream
500g asparagus

John Jenkinson, Evesham
Hotel, Evesham,
Worcestershire, UK

Cook asparagus in salted water, retain tips and puree the remainder

Bring the milk to the boil and pour onto the beaten egg yolks and sugar, return to the saucepan and cook until the mixture thickens, add the asparagus puree and cream, cool.

Churn in an ice cream maker.

Asparagus ice cream may be served as a savoury accompaniment. John says that it goes well with anything smoked, (especially salmon and smoked haddock risotto). It is also served on parmesan biscuits (made with melted parmesan).

Alfred Kinder, author of Asparagus

Evesham Gras

How does a grower cook his gras? Many growers boiled their gras with mint or sugar. Billy Byrd, from Bretforton, prefers his with salad cream but knows people might think that a bit odd. Locals suggest leaving a short length of woody stem to use as a handle when dipping it into melted butter.

Some Curiosities

Asparagus Ice-Cream and Sweet Dishes

Surprisingly, there are a number of recipes for asparagus ice-cream and one of the courses at a Bretforton Asparagus Ball was ice-cream too. There are many other sweet recipes especially from the US.

Other sweet dishes include:

- Asparagus Whip
- Asparagus Sherbet
- Asparagus Cheesecake
- Asparagus Fruitcake
- Asparagus Liqueur

On offer at the quirky Evesham Hotel, asparagus liqueur is in fact an *eau-de-vie* made from asparagus in France. Distilled at the Mette distillery in Ribeauville, asparagus *eau-de-vie* is something of an acquired taste as its bouquet is reminiscent of post-prandial visits to the smallest room!

Non-food Uses

Asparagus ferns can be used in flower decoration and a recipe for asparagus paper appears in Nancy Clarke Hewitt's book, *Asparagus: From Kitchen to Garden*.

Cooking Utensils

There are many cooking utensils that have been specially developed to partner asparagus. Some people are sceptical about their merits, preferring simplicity. The asparagus steamer is a vertical saucepan designed to boil or steam the woodier stems while gently steaming the tips.

Other kitchen equipment includes asparagus dishes and asparagus tongs.

Wine with Asparagus

Simply cooked, asparagus with its slightly sulfurous undertone and intense grassy flavour, can make many wines taste very strange. A crisp dry white such as Sauvignon Blanc or Pinot Grigio usually works but Chardonnay, which not only tastes vegetal, but also oaky, should be avoided.

Once incorporated in a recipe with a sauce or other ingredients it is these that may dictate the choice of wine.

I try to get them working. My older son is 10 and he's pretty interested. We had a dinner party the other night and he helped a lot. He helped peel asparagus; he hung out. It was great.

Todd English

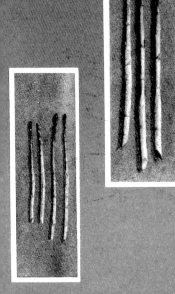

ASPARAGUS

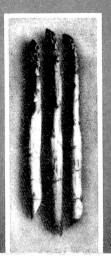

MINISTRY OF AGRICULTURE,

FISHERIES AND FOOD

BULLETIN N

Price 2s. 6d.

Asparagus Literature

Fred Archer (1992) *A Country Twelvemonth*. Sutton Publishing

Nancy Clarke Hewitt (1977) *Asparagus: From Garden to Kitchen*.101 Productions, San Francisco, CA

M Hexamer (1928) *Asparagus Its Culture for Home Use and for Market*. Orange Judd Publishing

Alfred Kinder (1947) *Asparagus*. Faber and Faber Ltd

Jan Moore, Barbara Hafley, Glenda Hushaw and Jacqueline Zupo (2003) *The Asparagus Festival Cookbook*. Celestial Arts

James N Parker and Philip M Parker, eds (2003) *Asparagus: A 3-in-1 Medical Reference*. Icon, ISBN 0-597-83780-5

Klena Raab (2001) *Cooking with Asparagus*. DuMont Buchverlag, Koln Dumont monte UK, London

Autumn Stanley (1970) *Asparagus. The Sparrowgrass Cookbook*. Pacific Press, ISBN 0-914718-22-3 1977

Recipe References

Details of individuals who have kindly made submissions to this book can be found with their recipe provided

Cold Sauces for Asparagus
Jane Grigson's Good Things, Jane Grigson, 1971. Michael Joseph/ Penguin Books Ltd. ISBN 0 141 469 01 3

Bacon and Asparagus Fraze
Fine English Cookery, Michael Smith, 1973, Faber, ISBN 0 571 111 28 9,

Petits Crèmes d'Asperges Sauce Maltaise (Little asparagus creams with Malaise sauce)
Restaurant Dishes of the World, Margaret Fulton, 1983. Octopus Books Ltd. ISBN 0 760 419 40 5

Asparagus Baked in Milk
The Best of Ukrainian Cuisine, Expanded Edition, Bohdan Zahny, 1994, Hippocrene Books, Inc, New York, ISBN 0 781 806 54 2

Asparagus and Almonds in Filo
"Times" Cookbook, Frances Bissell, 1993, Chatto and Windus, ISBN 0 701 145 43 9

Flemish Asparagus
World Cookery, author unknown, 1962, The National Magazine Company, Morrison and Gibb Limited ASIN B0000CLL97

Asparagus and New Potatoes Avgolemono
Flavours of Greece, Rosemary Barron, 2000, Grubb Street, London, ISBN 1 902 304 28 4

Marinated Asparagus
Flavours of Greece, Rosemary Barron, 4, 2000, Grubb Street London, ISBN 1 902 304 28 4

Asparagus with Polonaise Sauce
Charmain Solomen's Complete Vegetarian Cookbook, Charmain Solomen, 2002, Ten Speed Press, ISBN 1 580 084 27 3

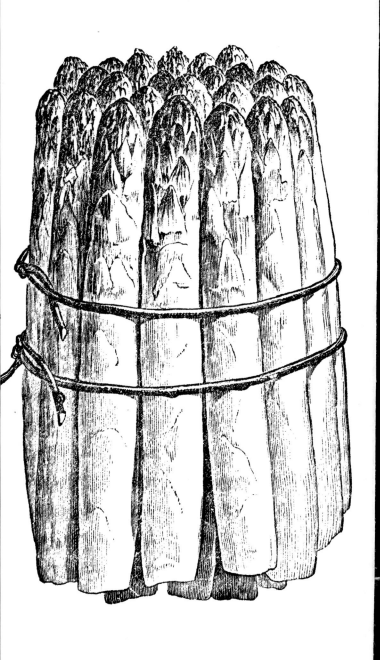

Quote References

p 12 'Saki', pen name of Scottish writer Hector Hugh Munro (1870-1916) [H.H. (Hector Hugh) Munro] Saki (1870–1916), Scottish author. Clovis, in "The Match-Maker," The Chronicles of Clovis (1911).

p 14 Jamie Oliver, Heart of England website, www.english-asparagus.com/id-37/Chef's-Quotes.html

p 19 Peter Ustinov, *Christian Science Monitor*, 14 November 1962

p 22 Pliny, source unknown

p 26 Prince William, 1982, source unknown

p 30 Rachel Green, Heart of England website, www.english-asparagus.com/id-37/Chef's-Quotes.html

p 32 JFK, 1917-1963, source unknown

p 36 Mario Batali, Restaurateur, source unknown

p 42 Sean O'Casey, Irish playwright,(1884 - 1964) Source unknown

p 46 Charles Dickens, Little Dorrit, Chapter 24

p 48 Cecil Beaton, On New York City, It Gives Me Great Pleasure John Day 55

p 54 Augustus, source unknown

p 59 William Gilbert, Poet, in the poem King Goodheart

p 60 Todd English, Chef, 1960, source unknown

p 66 Curly Howard, one of the Three Stooges, in "Busy Buddies"

p 76 Charles Lamb, from the essay Grace before Meat, Essays of Elia, published 1823

p 82 John Adams, in a letter to his wife Abigail

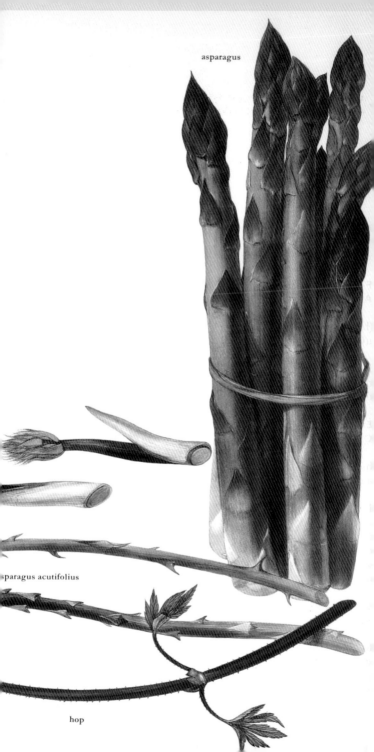

asparagus

sparagus acutifolius

hop

Other Resources

Evesham Asparagus website

www.eveshamasparagus.co.uk

Formby National Trust Archive

(http://www.nationaltrust.org.uk/main/w-ar4_e_form.pdf)

Fascinating accounts of life and times of agricultural workers from the last century.

Evesham Tourist Information Centre

http://www.evesham.uk.com/almonry.html

Based in the old Almonry, this centre has static displays of many asparagus artefacts. Just next door is a large 'gras' field where the crop may be bought in season.

Evesham Asparagus Festival – Angela Tidmarsh

Run for a number of years starting at the end of May, the Festival includes the famous asparagus auction, an asparagus ball and many other events. For more information, contact: Tourism Team, Wychavon District Council, telephone: 01386 565373

Email: angela.tidmarsh@wychavon.gov.uk

Badsey website

http://www.badsey.net/

Excellent community web site with many original letters, photos and other material.

Round of Gras Pub

http://www.roundofgras.co.uk/

The Fleece Inn

http://thefleeceinn.co.uk/home.html

Evesham Hotel

www.zen37209.zen.co.uk

Please send your comments and feedback on this book to Chris Sheehan at:

info@eveshamasparagus.co.uk

Acknowledgements

I would like to thank all the chefs, publicans, hoteliers, growers and locals who have helped make this book possible. Your unstinting generosity with time, recipes and tidbits of information have been invaluable. Thanks particularly to those who have submitted recipes to the book. I would especially like to thank John Jenkinson at the Evesham Hotel for his enthusiastic support of the project; Michael Barnard, local artist and historian, who has allowed me to use many of his unique drawings and who looked through the manuscript with a critical eye. Thanks to my reviewers, Chris and Barbara Ranger and John and Sue Jenkinson. And many thanks to Sue and Pete at the publishers Word4Word for their eye for detail, guidance and keeping me on track. All errors, as they say, are mine, however, I'd appreciate any comments via the email address listed in resources.